CW01459764

TRACTION ENGINES
PRESERVATION AND POWER

PAUL STRATFORD

HALSGROVE

First published in Great Britain in 2011

Copyright © Paul Stratford 2011

All rights reserved. No part of this publication may be reproduced,
stored in a retrieval system, or transmitted in any form or by any
means without the prior permission of the copyright holder.

British Library Cataloguing-in-Publication Data
A CIP record for this title is available from the British Library

ISBN 978 0 85704 092 3

HALSGROVE
Halsgrove House, Ryelands Business Park,
Bagley Road, Wellington, Somerset TA21 9PZ
Tel: 01823 653777   Fax: 01823 216796
email: sales@halsgrove.com

Part of the Halsgrove group of companies.
Information on all Halsgrove titles is available at: www.halsgrove.com

Printed in China by Everbest Printing Co Ltd

CONTENTS

Introduction   5

Engine Miscellany   6

Highways and Byways   41

'The Age of Steam' –
Nineteenth Century Survivors   67

Wagons Roll   78

The Farmer's Friend   88

Rolling Along   98

Set to Work   112

'Laid to Rust'   122

Engines Overseas   127

Back Home   136

INTRODUCTION

Since its inception the basic principle of using steam power generated by heating water in a boiler usually fired by coal has little changed. The earliest beam engines were used as pumping engines in mines, but were both costly to operate and were restricted in only having one power stroke per cycle. The partnership of James Watt and Matthew Boulton in the mid-eighteenth century revolutionized steam engine design with a double acting cylinder, and firstly using an epicyclic sun and planet gear system and later a crankshaft they were able to convert the fore and aft motion of the piston to rotary motion. This system became universal in not only stationary engines but also on the first steam tram and railway locomotives pioneered by Richard Trevithick and George Stevenson in the early1800s.

By the mid 1800s the portable steam engine with its cylinder mounted horizontally on top of the boiler was making headway into both industry and agriculture as a power source: it drove pumps, machine tools, threshing drums, chaff cutters and saw benches from a pulley wheel attached to the crankshaft to which an endless flat belt was attached. These portable engines required a team of horses to move from one work location to another.

It was Kent farmer Thomas Aveling who in 1859 modified a portable engine to create a self-moving agricultural engine that became the forerunner of the steam traction engine that we know today. The partnership of Thomas Aveling and Richard Thomas Porter in 1862 became known as Aveling & Porter, a company which went on to produce not only traction and ploughing engines but of course steam rollers – more than all other UK manufacturers combined.

Whilst steam railway locomotives lasted in revenue earning service on the national network until 1968, the demise of the steam traction engine began many decades before with the introduction of the internal-combustion-engined lorry and farm tractor, the steam roller and the odd pair of ploughing engines lasting in service little beyond the 1950s.

It is remarkable that unlike so many of our historical artifacts which are preserved and displayed in museums as part of a National Collection, the vast majority of steam traction engines are owned and maintained by private individuals and enthusiasts, but for whom our industrial steam heritage would be much the poorer. These enthusiasts have, for the most part without funding from Government or Arts Council grants, purchased, restored, maintained and preserved traction engines as an important part of our heritage. In addition to conserving these engines they are also preserving not only the techniques needed to safely run these engines but also the engineering and boilermaking skills required to maintain them both for the present and for future generations.

Aside from the fact that owners have a huge responsibility as custodians of these engines, there is of course another side – steam traction engine preservation is, after all, an enjoyable hobby which gives pleasure and a great deal of satisfaction to not only those involved directly, but to the general public at large.

How much longer will owners of traction engines be allowed to steam along our highways and byways and attend rallies? For sure, the enthusiasm and skills will be there, only future legislation will determine the day that the last fires will be dropped and all engines will be consigned to be lifeless 'stuffed and mounted' museum pieces.

ENGINE MISCELLANY

The engine line-up at the Gloucestershire Warwickshire Steam Railway Vintage Rally held at Cheltenham Racecourse is headed by Marshall Traction Engine *The Alderman* No. 28922 built in 1897.

The purposeful lines of Burrell Single Crank Compound No. 2426 built in 1901 are seen here against the backdrop of the Worcestershire countryside.

The ex-Anderton & Rowlands Fowler B6 'Super Lion' Showman's Road Locomotive *The Lion* Works No. 19782 built in 1932 waits patiently to begin generating at the annual Carter's Steam Fair at Pinkneys Green.

Opposite: Attending the Stradbally Rally in Co. Laois, Ireland is Fowler A4 General Purpose Engine No. 11031 built in 1907.

Arriving at the Bloxham Rally complete with living van and water cart is 10 ton Aveling & Porter Compound Roller No. 7600 'Victoria' built in 1912.

Opposite: Tasker B2 Compound Tractor No. 1424 built in 1910 spent part of its life converted to a roller but, as seen here, has now been rebuilt into the original tractor form.

Built by Garrett of Leiston in Suffolk in 1924 as a 4CD tractor No. 34461 'Victoria' was converted into a roller by Chris Lambert in 1944. Not until 1957 was the engine rebuilt by the Eastwood family into the original tractor form as seen here.

Opposite: Fowler and Road Locomotives are synonymous. This 6NHP class A4 example No. 9279 'Kitchener' built in 1902 passed through several owners in its working life, including the renowned Norman E. Box Ltd.

Burrell 6NHP Showman's Road Locomotive *'Earl Haig'* No. 3979 built in 1924 worked the West Country and London fairs whilst in the ownership of Symonds Cook of Gloucester.

Opposite: Unusual in appearance in having only a half canopy is *'Mr Potter'* a 4CD tractor built by Garrett in 1913 as No. 31633. Converted to diesel power in the 1940s the tractor was later restored back to original using parts from another derelict Garrett tractor.

Built in Lincoln at the Globe Works by Robey in 1927, Single Cylinder General Purpose Engine No. 42675 is seen here whilst attending a N.T.E.T. 'driving weekend'.

Ransomes, Sims & Jefferies Single Cylinder 6NHP General Purpose Engine No. 31100 built in 1920, at the Stradbally Rally, Co. Laois, Ireland.

Differing in appearance from the typical British-built traction engine, the 'Moose' was built in Canada by George White, an Englishman who emigrated to Canada and began making steam engines. The single cylinder engine was built as No.1198 in 1916, but only imported to the UK in recent years.

Built by Robey in 1924 as tractor No. 41492 for the War Dept. *'Bathsheba'* was converted for showland use in 1927. Seen here in a fairground environment at the Great Dorset Steam Fair.

Opposite: 1922-built Burrell Single Crank Compound General Purpose Engine No. 3919 *'Susie'* makes a spirited entrance to the Bloxham rallyfield.

Fowler 8NHP Showman's Road Locomotive No. 15653 *'Renown'* was built in 1920 along with sister engine *'Repulse'* for John Murphy of Co. Durham. In the autumn of 2003 *'Renown'* was extensively damaged in a catastrophic fire at the owner's premises, only to be totally rebuilt over a two year period back to her original immaculate condition.

Opposite: A Single Cylinder 7NHP General Purpose Engine No. 33471 built in Lincoln by Ruston Proctor in 1907, which spent all of its working life threshing and hauling in the eastern counties.

'Jimmie B', a Marshall Compound General Purpose Engine No. 34151 built in Gainsborough in 1900 is silhouetted against the setting sun at Hollowell.

Opposite: *'Little Mo'* a 6NHP Compound General Purpose Engine was built in Northampton by Wm. Allchin as No. 1652 in 1914. Pictured here at a N.T.E.T. driving experience weekend in Worcestershire.

Resplendent in the livery of its original owners, Messrs J.H.Herbert of Southampton, Burrell Showman's Road Locomotive No. 3890 'Majestic' built in 1921 stands proudly in the grounds of Belvoir Castle.

Fowler 'Duke of York', a 10NHP Crane Engine No. 17106 built in 1928, spent most of its working life with Marston's Road Services in Liverpool. Many photographs exist of this engine hauling huge loads of up to 120 tons in weight around the country. The engine was capable also of lifting and moving loads in excess of 15 tons using the jib crane. The name 'Duke of York' is recent and was given to the engine in 1952 by a former driver of the engine.

Marshall Compound General Purpose Engine No. 71837 built in 1919 was bought for preservation in 1959 for £90 and has remained in the same ownership ever since. Seen here at a Fairford Rally being steered by former champion jockey Willie Carson OBE.

Opposite: Built by Burrell's in 1913 for renowned West Country showmen, Anderton and Rowland, 'Lord Nelson' Showman's Road Locomotive No. 3443 is seen here preparing to generate power to drive the Ferris Wheel at a Gloucestershire Warwickshire Steam Railway Vintage Gala. This engine has since been converted to a Road Locomotive.

'Wait 'n' See', a 6NHP Burrell Three Speed General Purpose Single Crank Compound 'Aberdeenshire' Engine No. 2933 built in 1907.

Opposite: Aveling & Porter are better known as the largest producer of road rollers rather than manufacturer of road locomotives. *'Jimmy'* a class LC6 Two Speed 6NHP Road Locomotive No. 4561 built in 1900 is one of only a few surviving examples.

Burrell 6NHP Single Crank Compound No. 3665 built in 1915 is set against the magnificent backdrop of Berkeley Castle whilst attending the Lister Tynedale Rally.

Built in 1903, Ransomes, Sims & Jefferies Single Cylinder 6NHP General Purpose Engine No. 15127 'Winifred' spent its working life in Devon on threshing and haulage duties.

'Princess Royal' a Burrell 6NHP Compound Showman's Road Locomotive No. 3295 built in 1911, originally worked in England and Scotland before going to Ireland some forty years ago. They say that this engine has appeared in a number of films, but now is a regular exhibit at Irish rallies as seen here at Stradbally.

Burrell No. 3443 'Lord Nelson' was built in 1913 as a Showman's Road Locomotive for Anderton and Rowland. In recent years the engine was rebuilt as a Road Locomotive losing its showman's fittings and overall canopy.

Built in 1906 in Battle Creek, Michigan, USA by Advance Thresher as No. 7891, the engine was used for direct ploughing. The engine has been fully restored, being imported to the UK in 1977.

Two Fowler engines of a different stature are seen here at the Pickering Showground. Showman's Road Locomotive *'Prince of Wales'* No. 14948 was built in 1918 as a Road Locomotive for export to Russia but never delivered. After a working life in Hertfordshire the engine was converted in 1955 to Showman's specification as seen here. Beyond the Showman's Road Locomotive and smaller in all respects is Fowler T3 Compound Tractor No. 14406 *'Mtoto'* built in 1917.

Stanley Model 85 No. 5573 built in 1910 is a 25 HP steam car capable of 55mph and able to carry seven persons.

As are many traction engines these days, Burrell No. 3068 'Victory' of 1909 has been fitted with rubber strakes on the rear wheels and moulded solid rubber tyres on the front wheels making driving on today's hard-faced roads more comfortable for both engine and crew.

Burrell 6NHP Road Locomotive No. 3395 was supplied to J.Hancock & Son of Exeter in 1912 with a three quarter length canopy and finished in Crimson Lake livery. In subsequent ownership the canopy has been cut back and the engine painted green and for a time has carried the name 'City of Exeter' but is now named 'The Dalesman'.

Built in 1925 as a roller, Marshall No. 78667 was later converted to a traction engine and restored to its present condition from a kit of parts found in a farmyard.

Cresting the hill in the Heavy Haulage Arena at the Great Dorset Steam Fair is McLaren Compound Traction Engine No. 1534 built in 1917.

Marshall General Purpose Engine No. 5254 is silhouetted against the setting sun at the Great Dorset Steam Fair. Courtesy Yvette Stratford

HIGHWAYS AND BYWAYS

Marshall Traction Engine 'Margaret' No. 51025 of 1908 hauling both a support trailer and living van pass through the village of Cleeve Prior in Worcestershire.

One of the last Burrell Showman's Road Locomotives *Ex Mayor* No. 4000 built in 1925 shows a fair turn of speed through the Bedfordshire village of Gamlingay.

Ruston & Hornsby 12 Ton Roller No. 114059 built in 1921 is dwarfed by the magnificent backdrop of the Hook Norton Brewery in Oxfordshire. To this day the brewery still uses a Buxton & Thornley open crank horizontal steam engine to power much of the machinery in the brewery.

Fowler BB1 Ploughing Engine *'Achilles'* No. 15182 built in 1918 stands amongst a collection of vintage draglines in the yard of S.E. Davis and Son in Worcestershire.

Built in 1920 by Tasker in Andover as a light tractor No. 1822, the engine was converted to showman's specification in 1928. Now named *'Little Jim 11'* the engine is seen at an end of season road run in Clanfield, Oxfordshire.

Resident General Purpose Engine, Ransomes, Sims & Jefferies No. 26839 built in 1915 poses in the grounds of Eastnor Castle in Hertfordshire.

Opposite: Not what you normally expect to find at the National Exhibition Centre in Birmingham, a 10hp Model 65 Stanley steam car No. 7333 built in Newton, Massachussett, USA in 1913.

This 1893-built McLaren Single Cylinder Traction Engine No. 510 *'Phoenix'* was at one time converted to diesel power. In the 1970s a new boiler, cylinder and motion were manufactured to return the engine to its original form.

Preparing for an eastern counties road run in the grounds of the Royal Hospital School, Holbrook near Ipswich is 6NHP Aveling & Porter Tractor No. 11705 'Nippy' built in 1926.

Now fitted with rubber tyres over the original rear wheel metal strakes, Fowler K7 Ploughing Engine *'Linkey'* No. 14257 built in 1916, can now more comfortably travel along today's hard surfaced roads as seen here approaching the village of Inkberrow in Worcestershire.

On a beautiful spring day Burrell Single Cylinder 7NHP General Purpose Engine 'Rosemarie' No. 4088 built in 1930 passes along an East Anglian country byway.

The summit of 'Engine Hill' at Porthtowan in Cornwall is one of the most stunning locations to view traction engines on the road. Here Aveling & Porter AC6 Compound General Purpose Engine 'Elizabeth' No. 4157 built in 1898 takes part in the West of England Steam Engine Society Road Run.

Passing Lew Holy Trinity Church on an end of season road run is 1921-built Aveling & Porter 10 Ton Roller No. 9375 *'Bordon King'*.

Fowler class BB1 and class Z7 ploughing engines come head to head under a threatening sky in the village of Milton in Oxfordshire.

Opposite: With the village of Hook Norton in the distance, Fowler 7NHP General Purpose Engine No. 11699 *'Pride of Hanley Castle'* built in 1908 heads back to Chipping Norton on a beautiful autumn afternoon.

Burrell 5NHP Road Locomotive No. 3941 *'The Badger'* built in 1923 demonstrates the haulage capability of the engine, towing a trailer-mounted 'Lancashire' boiler over the River Avon Bridge in Warwick.

Opposite: Built in 1819 Thelnetham Windmill in Suffolk predates the Fowler A9 Road Locomotive No.15467 *'Sir Douglas'* by 101years. From 1892 until 1914 the mill used a portable engine to power an auxiliary pair of millstones.

Seen in the stableyard of Eastnor Castle are Wallis & Steevens Advance 10 Ton Roller No. 8082 built in 1931 and Foden No. 12770 built in 1927 as a wagon and now cut down to a tractor.

Opposite: Passing through the village of Littlebury in Essex is Ransomes, Sims & Jefferies 7NHP Single Cylinder General Purpose Engine No. 26995 built in 1916.

Passing through the Worcestershire countryside is Advance Rumely Two Cylinder Tandem Compound Engine No. 14291 built in 1914 in Michigan USA.

The historic church of St Mary in Cotesbach, Leicestershire provides the backdrop as Fowler Single Cylinder Ploughing Engine *'Aethelflaed'* No. 4223 built in 1884 heads out to the fields.

Built in 1913 as No. 3534, 'Monarch' was one of five 8NHP Compound colonial Road Locomotives built by Foden, the other four being exported. Seen here passing through Ipswich Docks.

Built in 2009 by Dawson Bros, under the Foster name, is Wellington Tractor No. 14741, the newest engine both on the rally circuit and on the road.

Whilst in the ownership of Arthur Napper, Marshall General Purpose Engine No. 37690 *'Old Timer'* built in 1902, became one of the best known of all preserved traction engines after taking part and winning the infamous race for a 'Firkin of Ale' at Appleford. Seen here on a more leisurely end of season road run near Hungerford.

Supplied new in 1917 to threshing contractors in Ireland, McLaren Compound Traction Engine No. 1534 returned to England in 2002 and is seen here on the owner's home territory of Cornwall surmounting the climb up from Porthtowan against the backdrop of the North Cornwall coastline.

Preparing to make a smokey departure from the courtyard of Eastnor Castle is Fowler B6 Road Locomotive *'Atlas'* No. 17105 built in 1928.

'THE AGE OF STEAM' – NINETEENTH CENTURY SURVIVORS

Aveling & Porter AC6 Compound General Purpose Engine 'Queen Victoria' No. 4255 built in 1899 enters the grounds of Stanway House in Gloucestershire amidst the colours of autumn.

The sole surviving ploughing engine No.110 built in 1870 by J.&F. Howard in Bedford. The engine is unusual in having the winching drum mounted horizontally across the rear and was originally designed for use as a single engine system of roundabout ploughing and cultivation. It was bought in 1929 and shipped to North America for display at the Henry Ford Museum in Dearborn, before returning to England in 1991 and restored to full working order.

Recorded as being the third oldest surviving McLaren traction engine in the British Isles, No.127 is a single cylinder 8NHP built in 1882 and worked in the same ownership up to 1963, mostly employed driving a sawmill.

Built in 1888 by Marshall of Gainsborough at the Britannia Iron Works, 6NHP General Purpose Engine No.16553 was exhibited at the Smithfield Show and was then sold, remaining in the same ownership for the next 59 years. Buried under a pile of scrap the engine was recovered in 1989 and restored to its present condition.

It is a remarkable fact that Marshall almost certainly has more surviving examples of pre-1900-built traction engines in the UK than any other manufacturer. Apart from portable engines, Marshall Single Cylinder 8NHP General Purpose Engine No. 14421 built in 1886 is the second oldest survivor.

Built in 1884 Burrell Single Cylinder General Purpose Engine *'Lord Burrell'* No. 1127 is the fourth oldest Burrell in the UK. Retained in Burrell ownership until 1905 the engine then spent the rest of its working life in the Cotswolds.

Opposite: The second oldest preserved Fowler engine in the UK, *'Margaret'*, a single cylinder 12NHP ploughing engine built in 1870, once owned by well known agricultural contractors Beeby Bros. of Rempstone. As with most older engines extensive restoration work has been carried out on *'Margaret'*, the boiler being replaced by Beeby Bros as early as 1920 whilst more recent restoration work was featured in the TV programme 'Salvage Squad'.

Not the oldest surviving roller built by Aveling & Porter in Rochester, but nevertheless still a fine example of a nineteenth century roller still in action today: built in 1894, 'Sarah' a 10 Ton Roller No. 3430 is seen here on an end of season road run in Gloucestershire.

Built by Burrell in 1887 and exhibited at the Smithfield Show, General Purpose Engine No. 15391 was sold to the Eynsham Hall Estate in Oxfordshire, where the present owner's grandfather was engine driver. Named *'Eynsham Hall'* the engine is seen here on a road run passing through Curbridge in Oxfordshire.

Little is known of the history of McLaren 8NHP General Purpose Engine No. 682 built in 1899, but in later years it stood at premises in Lincolnshire before being rescued for preservation and has appeared as an ongoing project at the Great Dorset Steam Fair for a number of years.

Opposite: Built by Shand Mason as a works fire engine for Watford Brewery in 1876 as No. 2017 and named *'St George'*, this horse drawn appliance is the oldest working Shand Mason in the world.

WAGONS ROLL

It is remarkable that this 1920-built Clayton & Shuttleworth 4NHP Box Van No. 48510 was unearthed in a derelict condition in a scrapyard in the 1970s and restored to this immaculate condition that we see today.

A regular visitor to the Great Dorset Steam Fair is Sentinel 'Super' Steam Waggon No. 7651 built in 1928.

Seen here entering the Castle Combe racing circuit is 'Island Chief' a Foden 'D' Type Tractor No. 12370 built in 1926, supplied to Arthur Kirby of Newton Abbot Sawmills whose livery the tractor carries today.

The only known survivor of 60 waggons built by Foster of Lincoln, No. 14470 was shipped to Australia in 1921. Discovered in 1983 the waggon was repatriated to the UK by the late Tom Varley and restored to the condition seen here. The waggon has since been further rebuilt as a tipper waggon as originally delivered.

Outshopped in the livery of its last owner before passing into preservation in 1959 is Sentinel Super Sports Tractor No. 7527 built in 1928. This tractor was first used by Sentinel as a demonstrator at their works in Shrewsbury.

Foden No.13832 *'The Dorset Wanderer'* was originally built in 1930 as a waggon but cut down and rebuilt as a tractor in later years.

Opposite: A very rare Ransomes, Sims & Jefferies 5 Ton Overtype Steam Waggon, in fact the only survivor in the northern hemisphere. Built in 1923 this 5NHP Compound Waggon No. 34270 was exported to Australia. Repatriated in 1999 the waggon has been totally rebuilt to the present condition.

Sentinel DG6 Steam Waggon No. 7966 was supplied new in 1929 to J. Lyons & Co. of London, the last and largest of 32 waggons they ordered. Believed only to have been in service for just 4 years, the chassis and body were recovered from a scrapyard in the 1960s. In its present ownership the restoration was finally completed in 2009 and must surely be one of the finest restoration projects to be seen on the rallyfield to date.

Opposite: Supplied new in 1928 to London brewers Fuller, Smith & Turner, better known as Fuller's, Foden 6 Ton 'C' Type Steam Lorry No. 13138 was used for deliveries in the London area. Restored to its original livery, the name *'London Pride'* comes from one of Fuller's leading brands.

'Yorkshire Lad' was originally built by the Yorkshire Patent Steam Waggon Co. in 1927 as a WG Type Chain Drive Waggon No. 2108, but was later rebuilt as a shaft drive WH type. The Yorkshire waggons are unusual in having a transverse mounted double-ended boiler with a central firebox and smokebox.

Built in Leeds in 1919 as No. 1365 by the Mann Patent Steam Cart & Wagon Co. Ltd for Beyer Peacock Co. Ltd, of Gorton Foundry, Manchester for general works duties. Parts of the waggon survived as a soil sterilizing plant in Cheshire before being recovered in 1989. An extensive rebuild followed using an engine unit discovered on Vancouver Island in Canada.

THE FARMER'S FRIEND

Fowler BB1 Ploughing Engine No. 15142 built in 1918 seen here in a farmyard in rural Worcestershire. Working as part of a pair winching either a plough or cultivator across the field, this engine was designated as a 'right hand' example as the wire rope exits from the right hand side as viewed from the footplate and when working the engine would be positioned on the left hand headland of the field and would operate in reverse gear.

In order to move from one ploughing job to another, the plough would be attached to the drawbar of the engine as seen here. In this scene, the engine is Wilder No. 1, constructed in 1926 by Wilder's of Wallingford using a boiler and cylinder block of their own design and further components from two redundant Fowler engines, bringing a balance plough into a recently harvested field.

Most ploughing engines were two speed, as can be seen here, the massive well-worn gear wheels transmittinng the drive from the crankshaft to either the winching drum or the rear wheels.

Opposite: The rope is drawn from the drum of Fowler Z7 as the plough is winched across the field by the opposite engine. The Z7 class engines were the largest to be built by Fowler at the Steam Plough Works in Leeds. This example No. 15673 was exported to the Sena Sugar Estates in Mozambique in 1922. Repatriated in 1977 and fully restored, this engine can often be seen at steam ploughing demonstrations or, as here, at a Steam Plough Club 'Hands On' weekend.

The sheer size of a ploughing engine can be appreciated in this rear three-quarter view of Fowler BB Class No. 14712 'Wilbur' built in 1917, whilst the flywheel of BB1 Fowler Ploughing Engine No. 15222 built in1918 is a blur as the engine winches a plough up the hillside at the Great Dorset Steam Fair.

Opposite: One of only two surviving Ploughing Engines built by J & H McLaren at the Midland Engine Works in Leeds is No. 1541 a12NHP Compound Engine built in 1918.

An amazing sight of four ploughing engines set ready for work, taking part in the Steam Plough Club Great Challenge held as part of the British National Ploughing Championships at Preston Capes in Northamptonshire.

The classic lines of a single cylinder nineteenth-century Fowler Ploughing Engine No. 1642 built in 1871 and worked along with No.1641 for many years by Beeby Bros. At one time Beeby Bros operated no fewer than eleven sets of Ploughing Engines from Dales Farm, Rempstone.

Fowler No. 15199 is one of a pair of BB1 Ploughing Engines supplied to Beeby Bros in 1918, but were converted to diesel power using Mercedes engines in the late 1940s and continued working commercially either dredging or mole draining until 1963.

Opposite: The parkland of the Shuttleworth College at Old Warden provides a tranquil setting for the smaller, less powerful class K7 Fowler Ploughing Engine No. 16646 built in 1926.

ROLLING ALONG

What better way to end the season than a road run on a sunny autumn day to the local pub. Ex Dingles Burrell Single Cylinder 10 Ton Roller No. 4012 *'Ventongimps'* built in 1925 is seen here in the Warwickshire village of Offchurch.

Arriving at the village of Eastnor in Herefordshire, having been driven from Great Malvern, is 1926-built Aveling & Porter Single Cylinder 8 Ton Roller No. 11467 'Viatect'.

A most unusual roller built by the Mann Patent Steam Cart & Wagon Co. Ltd, for light rolling and patching work has two front steerable rolls and a full width rear roll. Built in 1917 as No. 1145, the roller was originally sold to Kent County Council and was acquired for preservation in 1936, becoming one of the first engines to go into preservation.

Opposite: Fowler DNB Compound 10 Ton Roller No. 17492 built in 1928 is fitted with tar spraying equipment.

Wallis & Steevens Advance 8 Ton Roller No. 8005 built in 1929 is seen at the Fairford Rally in virtually 'as found' condition. The roller spent some forty-three years under a succession of tarpaulins before being sold to new owners who, whilst having replaced a number of mechanical parts, have retained the original patina finish.

Aveling Barford were one of the last manufacturers of steam rollers in the UK. Here an example of a 1943-built 10 Ton Single Cylinder Roller No. DTM 540 is seen in the grounds of Belvoir Castle.

Resplendent in Crimson Lake livery 1915-built Aveling & Porter Single Cylinder 10 Ton Roller *'Monarch'* is seen at the Moira Rally, an event which has sadly disappeared from the rally calendar.

'Jupiter' a 15-ton Aveling & Porter Single Cylinder Roller No. 8717 built in 1916 passes a traditional red postbox in the Oxfordshire town of Wantage whilst participating in an end of season road run.

Ex-Kenilworth Borough Council Fowler 10 Ton Compound Roller No. 15935 'Kenilworth' built in 1923 returned to its former home territory to attend the 'Town and Country Festival' held at the former Royal Showground at Stoneleigh near Kenilworth in Warwickshire.

Opposite: Supplied new to Coventry Corporation in 1938 this Aveling Barford 6 Ton Patching Roller No. AC 624 was sold into preservation in 1962 and has remained in the same ownership to this day. Seen here in the South Warwickshire village of Honington, whilst in the care of the author.

Having passed under the 32 arch viaduct on the Sudbury Line in Essex, Marshall Slide Valve 10 Ton Roller No. 74399 built in 1921 heads for the East Anglian Railway Museum at Chappel and Wakes Colne railway station.

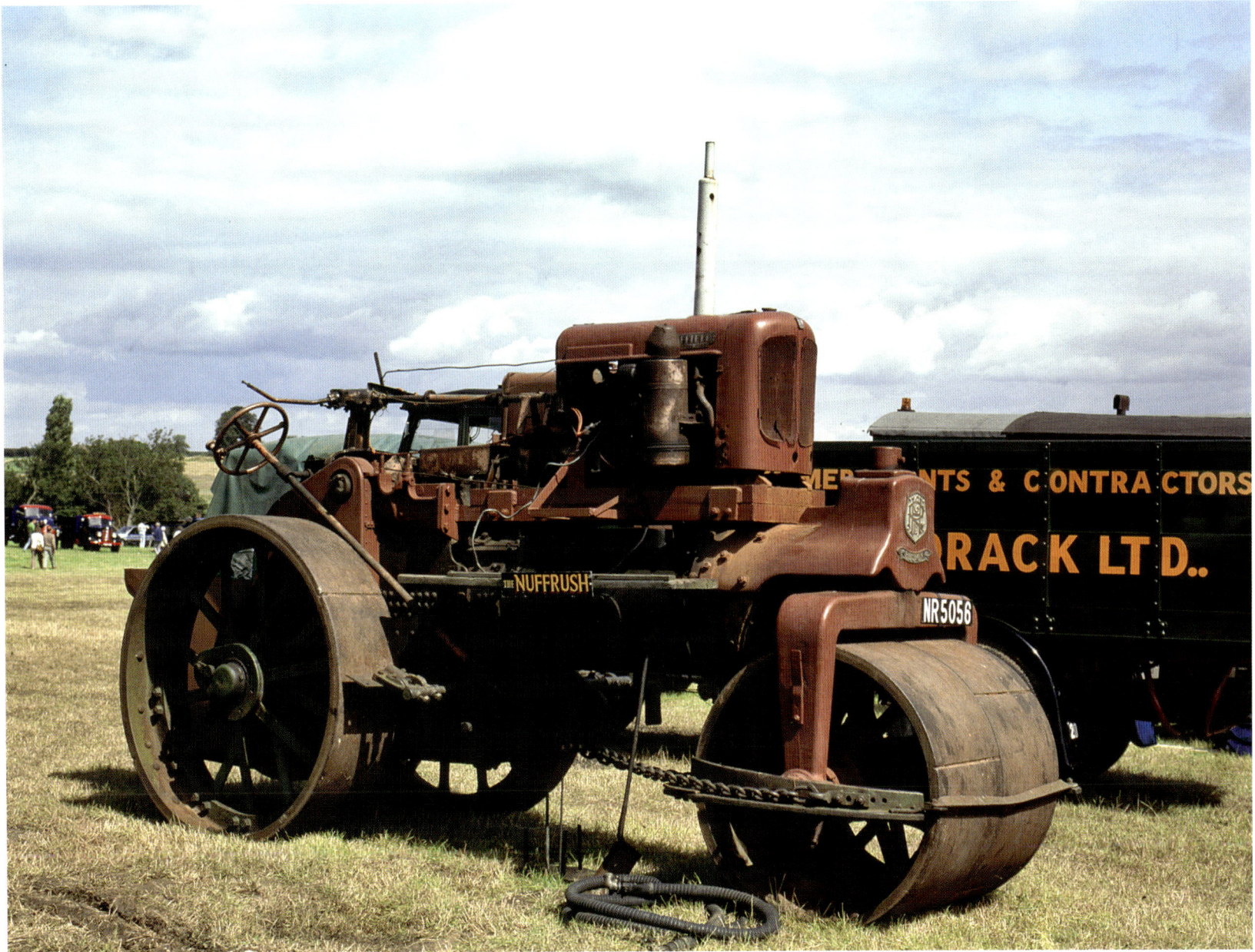

Having outlived its days as a steam roller the working life of this Ruston & Hornsby Roller No. 52694 built originally in 1919 has been extended by the replacement of the cylinder and motion with a Nuffield tractor power unit and given the name 'Nuffrush'!

Smiles all round as Marshall Piston Valve Compound 8 Ton Roller No. 76116 'Maid Marion' built in 1923 runs around the yard at Moira.

Opposite: Far removed from its starring role when driven by Sid James in the 1953 film *'The Titfield Thunderbolt'*, Aveling & Porter 10 Ton Single Cylinder R10 Roller No. 5590 built in 1904 poses for the camera against the backdrop of Berkeley Castle in Gloucestershire.

SET TO WORK

A re-creation of a scene commonplace in the 1930s, 1922 Fowler Single Cylinder DH 10 Ton Roller No. 14674 *'Busy Bee'*, formerly with Oxfordshire County Council, seen here scarifying the road surface near Cholsey.

Still in its original paintwork *'Pride of Devon'* a Burrell 5NHP Compound General Purpose Engine No. 4014 built in 1925 spent most of its working life threshing, but is seen here belted up to a racksaw at the Great Dorset Steam Fair.

Taking a break from a threshing demonstration is a Marshall 54 inch threshing drum driven by Garrett 4CD Tractor No. 33981 built in 1920.

The shape of things to come, an International Titan 10-20 tractor makes an appearance as 1884-built Fowler Single Cylinder Ploughing Engine No. 4223 *'Aethelflaed'* waits for the plough to begin its journey back across the field.

A matching pair of products from Foden of Sandbach working together at Kemble Airfield. The 1903 vintage Foden threshing machine is powered by *'Wattie Pollock'* a Foden 6NHP Compound General Purpose Engine No. 3384 of 1912 vintage.

Seen here at Sorley Cross against a backdrop of the Devon countryside, Wallis & Steevens 6NHP Single Cylinder General Purpose Engine No. 8052 built in 1930 was the last traction engine to be built by the Basingstoke firm. The racksaw is of circa 1920 and one of two built by A. Blake of Diptford in Devon.

The Marshall 7NHP Compound General Purpose Engine No. 52540 'Lorna' built in 1909 would have probably retired from its working life driving the Ransomes threshing drum before the 1958-built Nuffield tractor appeared on the scene. This threshing demonstration was captured on camera at a vintage working rally near Kingsbridge in Devon.

Opposite: The kettle is boiling on the brazier, the county surveyor has arrived in his Austin car to assess the progress at the roadmaking site, whilst 1904-built Aveling & Porter 10 Ton Single Cylinder R10 Roller No. 5598 '*Lady of the Manor*' simmers in the background.

Robey Portable No. 25961 of 1919 is belted up to the self contained combination apple 'scratter' and double cider press built by Workman & Sons of Gloucestershire in 1890 at the Burley Cider Making Weekend in the New Forest.

Opposite: On a sunny autumn day Fowler BB1 Ploughing Engine No. *15170 'Princess Caroline'* built in 1918 effortlessly hauls the huge four gang steerable disc cultivator across the stubble field.

LAID TO RUST

An unidentified Fowler Ploughing Engine is slowly succumbing to the ravages of brambles and vegetation in its resting place in a former contractor's yard in Warwickshire in the mid 1980s.

Seemingly abandoned, Aveling & Porter 12 Ton Roller No. 5683 built in 1905 lies amongst the undergrowth along with the remains of a Morris 1000 in a field in the West Midlands.

On a frosty morning three Fowler Ploughing Engines catch the early morning sunshine in a former Stratford and Midland Junction Railway yard in Warwickshire. These engines were converted from steam to diesel power with tender mounted GM Motors engines from Sherman tanks and were formerly used by contractors Bomford & Evershed for dredging.

Two Humphries Portable Engines lie under the hedgerow on a farmyard in Worcestershire.

Last used for lake dredging these two Fowler K7 Ploughing Engines Nos. 15133 & 15134 were converted by Maclaren with boiler mounted four cylinder diesel engines.

ENGINES OVERSEAS

In 1982 this unidentified Fowler Roller owned by Pakistan Railways is seen working in the station yard in Wazirabad, Pakistan.

Marshall Portable Engine 53976 built in 1910 preserved in a field near Maynell in the Orange Free State in South Africa.

Opposite: 'Texas Jack' a 1927-built Sentinel Super Tractor No. 7222 is preserved in the James Hall Museum of Transport in Johannesburg, South Africa.

Fowler Compound Roller No. 16480 built in 1925 is seen here preserved in Messina, a town in South Africa near the Limpopo border crossing with Zimbabwe.

Preserved in the border town of Messina, South Africa, is Ransomes, Sims & Jefferies Portable Engine 36119 built in 1925.

Fowler Compound Traction Engine No. 15677 built in 1921, classed as a TE 2 CO PE/TE double drum 'Farmer's Engine', possibly one of a batch built originally for export to France for use in vineyards is preserved in a museum in the town of Worcester, South Africa. Seemingly imported for ploughing it proved to be inadequate for the task and was replaced by a pair of Fowler Ploughing Engines, 15677 then being relegated to the less onerous task of dam construction and dredging. Restored at the South Africa Railway workshops at Salt River the engine was named 'Isobella', the original name being 'Ou Engeland'.

Opposite: Beautifully restored Foster Portable Engine No. 14529 of 1926 exhibited in the Kleinplasie Farm Museum in Worcester, South Africa.

A class AA2 Fowler Ploughing Engine No. 12095 built in 1909 and exported to South Africa, along with 12095 and a cultivator for use as 'harrowing engines' in the Koffiefontein Diamond Mine near Kimberley in South Africa. The engine is seen here at the Kimberley Big Hole Museum.

Opposite: In steam for an informal steam party being held at the owner's premises in Franschhoek, South Africa, is 1921-built Aveling & Porter Compound Steam Tractor No. 10096.

BACK HOME

Fowler Z7 Ploughing Engines Nos. 14367 and 14368 built in 1916 are two of six Z7s repatriated to the UK in 1977 after spending a working life at the Sena Sugar Estates in Mozambique. At the time that the picture was taken the pair of unrestored engines were waiting to go under the auctioneer's hammer, whilst in the background stands restored Z7 No. 15670 built in 1922. These impressive compound engines weighed in at over 22 tons and were rated at 22NHP with seven-feet diameter rear wheels.

Another engine repatriated from the Sena Sugar Estates in Mozambique in derelict condition and now fully restored is Ransomes, Sims & Jefferies 7NHP Light Agricultural Locomotive No. 36020 built in 1924.

After spending a working life in New Zealand, Foden 8NHP Road Locomotive 'Betty' No. 664 built in 1903 was brought back to the UK in the mid-1980s, fully restored and is now the second oldest surviving Foden traction engine in the UK.

Fowler type BAA 6NHP Single Cylinder Colonial Traction Engine No. 11717 built in 1909 is one of eight engines exported to Australia and referred to as 'Anglo-Australia' engines, spending most of its working life in New South Wales. At one time mounted on a concrete plinth, the engine was returned to the UK in 1992. After a lengthy rebuild the engine was first steamed again in 2005.

Opposite: Two McLaren Road Locomotives working in tandem, both of which spent their working lives in the southern hemisphere. Leading is McLaren 8NHP compound No. 1244 'The Emerald' built in 1911 and exported to Tasmania, returned to Ireland for restoration in 2002. Bring up the rear is McLaren 5NHP compound No.1497 built in 1917 and exported to South America, returned to Ireland in 2003 and completely rebuilt.

Built by Fowler as a B5 compound 8NHP Road Locomotive No. 9475 in 1902 the engine was exported to Australia and worked on an estate near Sydney on grain haulage and direct ploughing. Returning to the UK in 1978 the engine was rebuilt to showman's specification and named 'Duke of Rutland'. Seen here at Belvoir Castle, the home of the Duke of Rutland.

Opposite: An extremely rare Sentinel Super Two Speed Steam Tractor No.6426 built in 1926 and exported to Australia for work in a gold mine, mostly driving an ore crusher. Returned to the UK in 2006 the tractor has been extensively rebuilt including the rear-mounted winch.

Back home, but only for a brief visit, McLaren 8NHP General Purpose Engine No. 1242 built in 1911 and exported to South Island, New Zealand where it was used for threshing and contract haulage. The engine remained in the same family until 1969 when it was purchased for preservation. The engine was brought back to the UK in 2010 to attend the McLaren Special Event at the Great Dorset Steam Fair. Seen here whilst visiting the Bedfordshire Steam & Country Fayre at Old Warden.

Opposite: Two McLarens visiting the UK are seen here against the backdrop of the Shuttleworth College at Old Warden. 'The Pocket Rocket' was originally built as a 4NHP tractor in 1926 as No. 1835 but converted to a roller before being shipped to New Zealand. In 1969 began the conversion to tractor form as seen here today. General Purpose 5NHP Compound Engine No. 1266 was built in 1912 and exported to New Zealand, spending most of its working life chaff cutting. Both engines were on a brief visit to the UK to appear at the McLaren Special Event at the Great Dorset Steam Fair in 2010.

Built by Foden as Road Locomotive No.1423 in 1907 and exported to Tasmania, the engine was brought back to the UK in 1998 and rebuilt to showman's specification and named 'Storyteller'.

144